The Man
in the Green Chair

OTHER BOOKS BY CHARLES EDWARD EATON

Poems
The Bright Plain
The Shadow of the Swimmer
The Greenhouse in the Garden
Countermoves
On the Edge of the Knife

Short Stories
Write Me From Rio
The Girl from Ipanema

Critical Biography
Karl Knaths: Five Decades of Painting

The Man
in the Green Chair

by Charles Edward Eaton

South Brunswick and New York: A. S. Barnes and Company
London: Thomas Yoseloff Ltd

A. S. Barnes and Co., Inc.
Cranbury, New Jersey 08512

Thomas Yoseloff Ltd
Magdalen House
136-148 Tooley Street
London SE1 2TT, England

Library of Congress Cataloging in Publication Data

Eaton, Charles Edward, 1916–
    The man in the green chair.

    I. Title.
PS3509.A818M3   811'.5'4   76-46171
ISBN 0-498-02040-1

PRINTED IN THE UNITED STATES OF AMERICA

to Isabel

Contents

Acknowledgments

Harper's Magazine for permission to reprint "The Nude Poet."

Quarterly Review of Literature: "Memoirs of a Dandy."

Poetry Northwest: "The Wig," "Woman on a Sunporch," "The Masseur," "Blue Pool with Red Geraniums," "The Weight Lifter," and "The Man in the Green Chair."

The Malahat Review (Canada): "The Centaur."

The Antioch Review: "Madame Midget."

College English: "The Enfabled Nude," "The Goiter," and "Harpoon."

The Centennial Review: "Girl Raking Hay."

Perspective: "Homage to the Infanta."

Shenandoah: "The Pig," "The Barber," "Sun Helmet," and "Water Polo."

Concerning Poetry: "The Rose Hawk," "The Carcass," and "Little Sheba."

The Hollins Critic: "The Hypochondriac," "The Crow," "Nocturne for Douanier Rousseau," and "The Tattooed Lady's Collection."

Michigan Quarterly Review: "Neanderthal Memories."

Boston University Journal: "The Image on the Knee."

Acknowledgments are also due to the following magazines for permission to reprint one or more poems: *Choice* (Chicago), *New Letters*, *The Minnesota Review*, *The Denver Quarterly*, *Works*, *The Chelsea Review*, *Lillabulero*, *Ohio*

University Review, Kansas Quarterly, Red Clay Reader, The Critic, Yankee, Prairie Schooner, The Smith, Southern Poetry Review, Midwest Quarterly, Texas Quarterly, Forum (University of Houston), *The Canadian Forum*, and *Meanjin* (Australia).

Also, "Squashes," published in *Canadian Forum*, was reprinted in *Best Poems of 1969*, "The Wig," published in *Poetry Northwest*, was included in *Best Poems of 1970*, and "Sun Helmet," published in *Shenandoah*, was reprinted in *Best Poems of 1974*. Also included are parts of a long poem entitled "Five Études for the Artist" from the November 1972 issue of *Art International*. "The Model" was reprinted in the anthology, *New Southern Poets* (University of North Carolina Press, 1975).

The Man
in the Green Chair

1 / People in Parenthesis

Memoirs of a Dandy

Now that the world is like a spoiled soufflé
There's nothing to do but write one's memoirs,
The pneumatic thing, a reinflation.
No justification—Dear God forbid!
I abhor the ultimate self-denial.
I would leave one eye hanging on the grave,
One sleek hand encircling a luscious breast,
Two minor gifts, perhaps, for Everyman
Who so thoroughly misunderstood me—
Silk next to my skin and scented armpits,
A grape sliding slowly down the palate,
A fat hot-water bottle hung in mink:
Totally unfounded apocrypha—
I had an athlete running on my tongue,
A cautious banker listening to my pulse,
A soldier guarding Venus in his tent.
Since I abhor hyperbole, I pause
To say it much more simply—I pursued
Nothing to its bitter end. The athlete,
Banker, soldier met late at night and poured
The final nightcap down the burbling drain.
A hard workman lay in his pajamas,

An elementalist and gamekeeper,
Adjusting in his sleep the parting web.
One must learn to swing on a single thread,
Use it in the morning for a jockstrap—
I may as well confess no one mistook
Me for a dandy. I blurred the image
Just before it became too finical,
Cleaned the nose of the child with my own hand.
Who then was the real exquisite? you will say:
The man who did not wallow in abstractions,
The hard, almost brutal, self-surveyor?—
I have a little Venus in my garden,
Old, much used, lichened in her private parts.
There is a young man running through my mouth,
The sun's endless security at my feet—
You may employ these images to lift
One weightless spoon of soufflé to your lips.

Madame Midget

Her tiny heart, loaded with feeling close as a plum is to its
    stone,
Had to endure these great lumbering creatures
Who did not care how loose and large their lives had
    grown.

Even her husband, little imp, so lusty and yet so frail,
Had no notion of what she guarded in her tight, hermetic
    pit—
He spent his time, like all the big ones, holding up the
    flabby burden of the male.

14

Their loves, their pains, were large, they said, cherishing
   each oozing felon:
It did not matter when they stepped upon her tiny toe,
   burning like a pepper,
Or snatched her up and hugged her to a chest which hid
   a mushy watermelon.

Perhaps it was the fatal combination—little size and
   baited sex—
That even made her glad the large ones rode her
   husband on their shoe,
And coaxed him to the darling and disgusting exhibition
   of his tricks.

Let her face look like a peach if she could guard the
   plum—
Smaller by an inch, or just above Goliath's knee, she
   would not yield her pith
To any mincing little toad or massive, minatory bum.

What did she have in her heart?—What gave the lot of
   them the right
To ask if it were seed within a seed, congealed, a pearllike
   tear,
Or some unearthly brilliance she had pressed from their
   prerogatives of light.

The Brothel

In the brothel the man hoped to recover
All the colors of the rainbow. Out of
His belly the boomerang would burst

As if the women made him gleam and arch.
He would plunge and toss and then let them roll
Over him, a malleable arc pressed fresh
Again in several colors. His lungs would fill
Like flowers taking in the sun and air,
And his eyes lose their moving marble cast.
The question of compassion was touch and go.
One woman would not do—he must be free
To pick and choose as from a bonbon dish
Or, if he wished, they must hump themselves in drifts
Around him, and he could lie there in siesta,
Dreaming that the spring poured down to him
All scents, all flowers. In a pneumatic bed
He then might take a book of lyrics in his hand
And read of love until they drowsed and lounged,
Complaisant as daughters of Proserpine.
Putting his socks upon his stark white feet,
He would suddenly feel the color rise in him
And he might walk outside, one great tattoo,
Not minding collars, ties, the whole trussed world
Whose threadbare myth would seem to him rewoven.

The Eunuch

Men despised him but trusted him with their wives,
Those sleek bitches with lewd gems in navels—
Just to be near them gave him hives.

He could tell they would prefer virility
In him as if an old well suddenly gushed water
Or a green branch sprouted from a long-dead tree.

He wanted to please but could not help being cruel,
Pulling a run in their silks or bumping their hips
Until he heard a ring upon the floor of a moist and
  aromatic jewel.

How is it to be the keeper of a thing best spent?—
He must tuck in their jewels again,
Anoint their soles, mend each little rent,

Let them doze like gauzy melons on the boards,
A ripe underworld of unfulfilled desire
Until the men come in jangling phallic swords.

He cries out for them, but they do not scream
When the world is jolted together by those crude smiths
And the gorgeous burning jewel throbs an exclusive
  dream.

The Wig

The short woman wearing the foot-tall wig
Who seems to have usurped a yellow hive
Suspects this is not the head's true home:
Her eyes will sometimes light with suppressed wings,
She fears mauling hands as if they were a bear's—
Only the passion to be someone different
Steadies her, and the knowledge that the brain
May well be incubating under hair.

So now her thoughts will have a yellow home;
They can come and go, well pollinated—
There is synergy among her wishes.

17

One can almost sense the comb being filled.
We must stand near her, let the spirit hum,
Never regret the thousand flowers drained:
The dynamo beneath the cotton candy
Could have a revolution well in hand.

It may be sad at night to see the wig
Faceless on its form, no longer alive
With transformation, but this is the price
We must pay for such a revelation—
The woman asleep looks gray, passionless,
Tubercular with terror—Ecstasy
That set the cowl could not reveal the brain,
Lucid, thick with amber, crawling with bees.

The Hypochondriac

The man sitting in his bed had had his legs broken
By women, by beauty, the ecstatic perfume in the
    garden—
Even now the women sat around his bed as if he were not
    sick but only recently awoken.

In their pastel stockings, miniskirts, they looked like
    flowers pressed in the future's album,
Little girls who had loved their father who had forsaken
    them,
And now he had asked to see them for a last time, and
    they had come.

It was hard to tell whether the place was clinical or
    gracious, hospital, hotel.

18

This is always the problem of depredations in a sensual
place—
Is it better to sicken with what one has truly had, or rally
and get well?

One girl in yellow with green stockings bloomed like a
jonquil—
They had been obsessively in love and now she would
envase herself
Like a cut flower sucking at the water of his will.

Such quiet, stuffed places as these need never be too
much.
Stalled passion is a virile thing forever,
Hides its own tableau of the body swinging down the
street like a knife, each arm upon a crutch.

One rests in memory, adores its illness, faded happiness,
Only to rise and ride the wild horse with two wooden legs
As if it did not know the destination of this freight of
glamor and caress.

The Evening Dress

When she put it on, a mythic serpent dressed itself—
The great applelike flowers and the glistening foliage
Had the overpowering scent and force of legend.
When is a woman more potent than when she arms
Herself for evening? She is all that she is
And all that she has dragged forcibly out of the backward
slide.

Thus she imprints herself with what she once
Could not withstand. Those green and apple colors
Are the smears of her long journey through the night.
Here at the glossy summit of nocturnal power,
Her pointed fingers, sashed-in flesh, the swirling,
    upswept hair
Tell us that she twists the secret rope of being.

The golden night rung dry for pleasure,
The clamorous bells played then silenced by her hand,
Mimics, challengers, implacably rebuked—
The man who spills a glass of wine upon her dress
Will see it as the splashed chimaera of his suicide
Or a hidden birthmark he hazards to transfer.

The world's walls may look queasy, but this rich column
Stands, her torso marbling in the chill of night.
That fruited serpent gown is her redress
For having been misled, repeatedly seduced—
It is the rope espaliered in sleek skin,
The exuded dream whereby all beauty may prevail.

The Enfabled Nude

Steeped in the mutilated, flawed world, what more can
    make us wince?—
The loathsome toad does not want to become a lithe
    young man:
He has seen with bulging eyes what happens to a prince.

The fable is so sleazy, unpredictably given to backlash—
One can be toad, prince, and back again within an hour,

And time seems hardly more than a vomitorium for our
  personal trash.

So we take the warts-and-all, the hard-line view
Only to see some microscopic, silken patch of skin
Suggest another culture breathing in the very worst we
  do.

A singsong history pertains: poor prince, poor toad:
There is not enough elegance left for a masked ball,
And tragedy wants one costume at a time, and that one
  poorly sewed.

What can one do but interchangeably remember and
  forget?—
I have spent years dressing down to meet the prince
And dressing up to handle with some charm my
  bumptious pet.

There are days, though, discarded skins and costumes
  steep the floor—
Naked of meaning, one longs to compress the flaccid
  fable
And say to metamorphosis: I will not rise to your
  occasions anymore.

2 / Life Styles and Labels

The Pig

He can be comic, tragic, loathsome, endearing, all in one,
The little figure toothpicked with cocktail sausages,
A malevolent, fat, eunuch-creature, ore-eyed in the sun.

We prefer, of course, the old homestead feeling of there
    on the hoof goes ham—
It surmounts the pigsticking, it even survives
All of our processing—from this death, we still make
    Spam.

But we console ourselves for all our vast pollution and
    our slops—
No matter that we raise him in the muck and mud,
The corpse is savory, and we have our chops.

Take the impeccable Idea—we shall have our world as
    Will:
A catchall for almost anything that anyone conceives,
The pig is a tumor trotting in the yard, happy to be fed
    on swill.

To some rough breeders, I suspect that any boor or prig

Can be seen as a thing to be fattened on refuse,
  processed, sold,
And, as one pushes away all evil from oneself, named
  "Pig!"

Poor pig, poor perjured thing that you and I may yet
  become,
Blanketed in sulphurous smog, an amalgam of food
  and death,
Our eyes leaking the smelted drop, each other's scorned,
  but indispensable factotum.

Purple Dwarf, White Lilacs

The man stands powerfully among white lilacs,
Glad the purple are in another part of the garden:
They hang in the distance like so many damaged,
  much-used punching bags.

He is a white champion now, clenched knuckles, sure of
  himself, no holds barred.
He has gone in for the kill of opposing dreams so many
  times
And lives, hermetically strong, entirely in a world of *fait
  accompli*.

He means to keep it this way, everything stripped down
  to tough, white skin,
The lilacs themselves, distilled, 100 proof, heady as white
  lightning—
Such a bizarre athlete has by no means had his day.

The dwarf in a dress the color of grape soda comes up
  the drive,
Waddling, rolling her bunched hips in an invisible bog.
Is this white lilac country, sonny boy? she asks.

I tell it to you as from one to whom it might have
  happened,
The man who knows the last purple punch has never
  been thrown:
There it is on the ground, in female form, full of fizz.

Something, somewhere, always retains the disavowed,
  discarded juice.
The dwarf looks like a contained jet, a beleagured,
  delaying action.
The man must get down on his knees to deal with her at
  all.

Otherwise she looks between his legs as through a windy
  Arch of Triumph,
A little, potent, charged, savage princess on another
  level—
He falls to his knees with something like a long orgasmic
  sigh.

I tell you this, having known the terrible, dangerous
  swoon:
This is what it is, the mercury of another being in your
  veins—
Dank with color, the man must rise, spread his legs for all
  the purple horde.

Woman on a Sunporch

He is holding her breasts, the golden man,
He is kissing her lips, stroking her thighs,
And yet no one in the world can see him—
He carries a can of light golden paint;
When they are not busy making love he
Is always engaged in lucid repairs.
Give him a cracked brown vase, an old dream-jug:
He will make it overflow with honey.

She knows he will stripe her like a convict
If she covers herself with refusal:
A strange barred woman haunts her in her bath.
And yet he works all over without mark,
His kisses overprinting one another.
The white eye shadow which sunglasses leave
Is the one weary touch saved for the last,
The blanched sophisticate her mind conceals.

So little really takes us in this world—
The skin has mainly patched and blotchy days,
The dressing room reveals our bandages,
The rolled tan stocking yields a plaster-cast—
We indulge the woman on the sunporch
As though she had the only private room
That counts—Her secret lover generates
A bloom that means to paint the peeling brain.

The Cowboy

The thing that made him seek his life recedes
While he stays put—To some, an actor, to those who love
  him
A virile, understated Pan still playing on his reeds.

But the land will not stay tied, moves
Always into background as if he were mastered by a
  photograph
Which puts him in the close-up's void while his own
  world roves.

We observe him minutely like a coin in hand,
Held up, an eye that once saw Sitting Bull
And saw the Indian, too, grow vague and distant from his
  land.

One might become vagrant if one were not used to these
  mishaps,
And roam, roam, roam beyond the coin's eye
To meet under the chaparrals the horny-handed man in
  chaps,

Seeing the cattle come up like subjects of a king,
Smelling the dust, the earth itself, as his aroma—
Glimpse the ceremonial little fire, hear the bacon sizzling.

This is the way we grapple, this is the way we knock out
  part of the sky
Where the land can pour thickly through forever—
This is where we force the buffalo beyond the nickel's
  eye.

The Gigolo

The gigolo was pink and charming, but as the years
   passed
He felt as if his face wore stark white makeup.
The women said he was pink and charming,
But when he undressed he felt costumed by lust
Covering him with body-hose like grease paint,
The condom he put on, a white balloon.
And they lay there, languorous, smoky,
Made up of stretchable integuments,
Ready, by extension, to be inflated.
He was a stripped clown among circus stuffs:
Everything depended on a male performer.
Then at his best he was the acrobat,
Sweet as a death-wish, half-stretched in white,
Thrusting up through tights, virile with leaves and
   tendrils,
Bounding from the net to plant the one and only Tree of
   Life.
But late at night when the seamy show folds up,
His heart must roar, his hands threaten them
With paws, their stockings and their garter belts
Lying like parts of a tent suddenly ripped through.
He is too tired to be the tamer now,
Just the wary beast violently at large.
And this is what they pay him for, to stay
Pink, charming, and inspire them with vicissitudes.
One woman, then a troop, a ring—he has
A circus life that's cotton-candy-kissed,
His moods all spun for him upon a spool
Until a white face in the blue mirror

Looks darkly backward where a gashed tent bleeds,
Yards and yards and yards of women lie,
And he can dream of being wrapped in all their gossamer
Like a Pharaoh swaddled in the clothes of concubines
Or a man with total burns sleeping in the light.

The Masseur

Is there a woman underneath this woman?
Can we make this flesh come true? The masseur
Thinks we can—Believe in him as your optimist.
Is there a murky staircase in your bones
Which leads to where a prisoner is kept?
The masseur knocks upon a thousand doors,
Waiting to receive as visitors just those
Sluts he takes one hard look at and evicts.

The masseur considers himself with no
Small arrogance tough as a master builder
Among the soft tenements of women—
In his tenderer moments, the only
Artist privileged to work in flesh.
But there is always the hard, resourceful
Earth with its stairway made of flattened stones,
The beautiful clear click of steps descending.

"Do we truly make the world by force?" asks
The masseur. "Is it a made thing or found
Forever lying in the kidnapped flesh?"—
At any rate we start with surfaces.
Working with beauty oils upon his hands,
He croons, "I am the man who musters legions.

I mean to pinpoint just the tight-clenched locus
And listen to the footsteps going down."

The Sailor

Wearing a map of lurid travels on his skin,
He will let his sweetheart read his life in love,
And let her think he's learned a different kind
    everywhere he's been.

Not exactly the secret of the universe like Queequeg,
But his brown, supple skin will look to her full of
    transfers, rolled
By moist, staining hands, back and forth across the bed,
    as though it were an Easter egg.

Violent and gratuitous acts of love do not necessarily
    demean
The sailor in the lover's eyes. Perhaps it is a virtue
Of the sea itself that seems to keep the well-impassioned
    clean.

Most sailors dress in white—When they disrobe,
Only the bold topography of life remains,
Ineluctable for lovers who see him turning like a globe.

Still, only the sweetheart knows how to stop him with a
    smile
As if she found a mystery saved for her, and said:
Let us pause in this blue country for a while.

And yet it seems a time to sleep, a lovely way to nap and
  doze,
The sailor in her body's hammock hung, as if any
  moment now,
Roughly turned over, out of love, he will grab his socks
  and clothes.

Blue Pool with Red Geraniums

Let us indulge in a restful, rigid exclusion,
Let us make a simple postcard of our lives,
If you will, a kind of pornographic, intense observation.

The pool and the geraniums seem to cooperate
As if they had been photographed over and over out of
  context,
Allowing anyone to say: Wish you were here—and not
  mean it.

We will provide the stud and the bellydancer—
That is all we want to say to the world today,
Just give us the bluest pool, the reddest geraniums,

And we will do the rest, provide the show.
We want to be a lewd illustration in our own minds,
We want to have broken off a piece of the world.

It does not matter if the book has only one page
As long as it is blindingly illuminated, blue and red,
And the bodies never become staid and statuesque.

Nevertheless, a voyeur inevitably appears, our first
  reader.

We cannot beat back his avid, Cyclopean eye—
He points out that the geraniums look rather
  blood-soaked,

The pool might be the place a harem dyed its veils.
He is an enormously inventive assimilator
And plans to tuck us, still protesting, in his large
  loose-leaf book.

Will there be a place to hide among so many fantasies?—
Our story had charm, was not meant to be encyclopedic,
All middle, no beginning, no end, until the Cyclops came.

3 / Infants and Invalids

The Goiter

The woman would say her throat was giving birth—
And—bless her wit—stroking that white belly,
She made no bones about increase, month by month, of
   this parturient girth.

Her body simply did not like the status quo,
The conventional love life that most swan necks have—
Something must rise and show the world how it sustained
   the sexual blow.

No doubt at first she could have worn, in subterfuge, a
   choker
Until it pressed and pressed its life against the pearls:
The child to be was like a belly dancer—and hands must
   stroke her.

There in the middle of the throat the torso of "La Source"—
How, without becoming preponderantly pathological,
Can we submit and let the morbid run its course?

One, without any doubt, can live in purdah and reveal

The glimmer of the much more fleshly thing beneath the
   veil,
Or put in some full form of art or wit an odd allusion to
   the way we feel.

One wished the woman good delivery and *bonne chance*—
I have known the stifled, coursing, feeling and wondered
   where the wit was
Which contemplates the body in its rankest terms and
   gives the little belly leave to dance.

Enfant Terrible

That day of his death, the wind blew,
The sky was wildly clear, devoid of clouds.
His mother and his sisters could not cry,
His brother cursed the phantom-father holding back
The rain. I, alone, had known the brother, son.
I will not match him with their hoard of parts:
The red-gold hair, the mouth like a plum-smear,
The eyes whose vision was turned inside out,
Looking at a tarnished mirror on his brain—
I say I knew him when I only saw him,
Booted, leather-jacketed, obscure,
His soft body shaped from Eve's white leavings,
The man-child Adam might have made if he
Had made one at the time—That was a clever theft,
That was a beautiful hand-me-down in history
When he took himself from all the others except me.
It required a certain genius to rely on me
Who never took a single path he took,
Who watched him cross the plaza, doll-like,

As we watch a gunman sequestered on a film.
He looked up, smiled, as if he did it all for me.
I almost cried out: Stop! But then the fascination
Held, a plush red carpet self-unrolling there.
I like smokers, drinkers, obsessed pornographers
If they do not twin and bind me to their lives.
And he who held me at arm's length himself
Knew that I also made the world for him.
It was the coming close that made it all so hard,
It was the fearful handshake that might weld.
I could have told him the bottom was not gold,
The axle of his nature could not rut the mire
To jeweled pavement. Under nothingness, a nothingness,
And only a grasping upwards for the sill
That once had looked on orchards blooming,
The delicate blossom-fruit-death charade
Which something that loves surfaces enacts.
But he would not have believed me, nor I
Except as I fevered when the picture died—
There is no one in the window, but someone walks
The plaza all alone as if he did
Eternal penance for a pair of eyes.

The Centaur

Is it the silky, hairy underpart wanting to be man
Or the upperpart desiring celerity and the charm of
    abandonment
That makes this myth coming toward us spiritually risky,
    catch as catch can?

The underpart in everybody's mind stays just the same

As if a horse were created forever satisfying
And with the upper reaches of nature only, we would
    play our perpetually fantastic game.

You can place yourself, any number of men, your
    favorite foolish modern guru
On all that solid, moving, powerful, ineluctable beauty,
And the horse, the horse, at least stays true.

But the face can change, wild as a prophet, sad as a child,
Feeling its tangled hair to see if the silk is coming up and
    through:
You fear the horse moves on, fiercely pure, and will not
    be reconciled.

You detach your head and shoulders like a plaster cast
But have nowhere to set them. The graft did not take:
The horse lives, runs into the future, refusing to leave his
    limbs in last.

The world looks like a sad-sack studio of interchangeable
    upper parts,
Old heads, fixed staring eyes, and the long stiff arms
    hanging down,
Saddled over the strange, carted-away presence of
    whatever contains our hearts.

The Woman with the Scar

Though it was a birthmark, she always said
A lover left it there in an insane fit
Of jealousy, just beyond the nostrils,

As if her nose had been transplanted—
"It was an act of discrimination,"
She would say, or, since it was purplish,
"I pushed my face in lilacs—they cut me."
It took a while to get used to her bizarre
Remarks, the risks she took with everyone.
Sometimes she tempted you to reach out
For the blade in her face and strike at her
With some dark, hallucinatory love.
But her whole body would close, a full-length knife,
Its blue edge offered to your tingling hand.
These Picasso-faces were conceived long ago.
It is better to think of them as wearing
A narrow window like a stained-glass wedge,
Not to be looked in too closely.
So she wears lilac, absurd strings of beads,
Lifts a smoke screen with a constant cigarette,
Loathes the *bienaise* you would inflict
Like a one-way window hidden in a wall—
One dreams of her nude, unblemished body,
The violet gown that flutters down like shadow,
Caught on the hook of that scar, her hand flung
Up to ease the garment tender as skin.
You wake to know that you must pick your way
Through slivers of glass to that deep window,
Naked, twitching your body like a robe,
No socks, nothing to guard the genitals,
To find yourself cold, thin as a slide,
As she inserts you in a magic lantern
To see if you project a purple light.

The Brass Bed

The bronzed couple are incestuous twins
The brass bed gave birth to an hour ago;
They are twisting tubes of gleaming metal—
I come to the age when such an image
Thrusts without warning into the hard mind,
Commands a bleak, obligatory tone.
Yes, indeed, the lovers strike a harsh gong,
The dependent man, receptive woman.

Quite naturally a mirror on the wall
Must perform as an aid to memory.
It silvers their limbs a little, suggests
A slight softening of cold geometry.
There was another conception somewhere:
The brilliant tubes run with sparkling water,
I see two naked figures in the rain.

Then why do I tolerate the brass bed?—
Why do generals wear medals in peacetime?
Certainly the world does not lack scrap metal,
The bold bed does not mean to go that way.
I will lie down and, there, you will lie down,
White as snow, ready to melt with feeling—
We would have sold the brass bed long ago
If refuse were not stolid in its grandeur.

The Barber

Having experienced the large view, one would like to see
  the pores,
Magnify the unmagnifiable sea, examine
The skin of a blue man, stretched out for inspection, as
  he snores.

How did one ever think of such a thing? What gives?
  What's up?—
The image of the blue man prone and your small white
  face peering down
While the foam lathers an epidermis in a barber shop.

One has to go on with it. One is committed, stuck,
Unless you want to slit the plump throat of a florid image
And say: No dice this time, old man. You're out of luck.

Still, language loves a surgical, oddly bumbling
  atmosphere,
Holding up its throat a little tensely as if you were part
  quack,
Just a barber to whom skin was something he must keep
  bland and sheer.

Nevertheless, a perilous understanding, a dubious
  entente—there is a knack,
A domination, and yet a gift of sensuous massage,
Which makes a tonsor of the sea not altogether like a
  hack.

You have handled flesh with and without mercy when it
  was flabby, tight,

Examined the pores, used an astringent, only to give back
The stimulated skin to that blue man sleeping in the
   light.

The Weight Lifter

Impacted with his own strength, the weight lifter
Abhors the notion of weightlessness—
Anything too light makes his body float:
Even pencils should be heavy as crowbars.
Tell him your mood is low, he will lift it;
Will him your quick, ethereal brain,
And he will bronze it like a baby's shoe.

Circumstances conspire to make us what we are.
The weight lifter knelt to the boost as to his fate
And muscles pushed beneath the flesh like bulbs—
This was what it was to have a body
Packed with the controlled thrust of daffodils.
Like the slow, silent lifting of the earth,
It begins in his feet, shifts pebbles, then rocks:·
There's ecstasy in the heavy head of things!

Having derailed the caboose, lifted the wheels,
He makes his move with mechanic things,
Content as a hinge, ceaseless and grotesque.
He, alone, remembers when perfection,
Swollen, sacrificed itself to the obscene,
Static, inaccessible to women,
Jaundiced through strength, in a land with no myths.

Siesta with Rapid Eye Movements

—And so to lie down as though in arabesque:
Flowers, foliage, fruits, animals, lounging dancers in
   silver mesh,
So vulnerable and yet without a dampening hint of risk.

How potent we are, how loaded with our lives
When we recline among the things we love,
Letting some other hand cut the flowers, pare the
   glowing fruits with knives!

The arabesque lies scattered everywhere—
We live in a disorderly house, we are people of ill fame,
The police will enter at any moment and literally strip us
   bare.

It is in foreknowledge of that impending raid you lie
Naked, the girls meshed in the fabric of fountains will
   attend,
Your lidded body safe behind the door like a calm and
   sleeping eye.

Unsurprised among your riches you will be superbly
   found—
The cached and loaded life is the one great answer now
As if one did not know the reputation of the flesh was
   ruined.

You will refuse to accept the charges, refreshed by
   dreams, for such they were,
Uncull the fruit, the flower, release the dancers through
   the harried house,
And catch the unwarned, wayward child sliding down the
   banister.

4 / Quotations from Corvus

The Crow

Can't we be bright like the flamingo, pure as the snowy
    egret?
The crow said no—he wasn't going to let us get by on
    color and form:
It was the lice, the mud on the feathers, we must not
    forget.

That girl in shocking pink who struts like a flamingo
Is on her way to being a garish soubrette, and who is
    there to say
It's the nitty-gritty, stretched-out facts of the case she
    ought to know.

Yes, I have seen a company of egrets fleecy as cloud,
But, egret by egret, have you considered the mood of the
    bird
Who, before he becomes extinct, may be thought of as
    wearing a shroud?

I walk in black and I should be your solemn fowl—
I eat the corn, disturb your morning rest with such a caw
As should reduce your claims upon the real to something
    quite subliminal.

If you persist, standing like a foolish feathered muff on
   reedy legs,
Or drooling lacelike plumes destined for a lady's hat,
I shall remind you, in the end, it is the elegant poseur
   who begs.

How can we make our dialogues more meaningful, our
   confrontations less absurd?
Quite shaken, the flamingo-egret complex was ready to
   concede, combine—
The crow said no: You belong to me for keeps, but I am
   not your bird.

The Rose-Hawk

The man seemed to be flying the hawk
As he stood in the rose garden looking up.
Veering with the wind, it looked like a kite,
Never lost from the string of his attention.

It toyed lazily with his human notions
Of fixity, ironic about centers, loci—
Let the man suppose that a downdraft
Would ensure the circling of the rose garden.

Let him think the roses were magnetic,
Hawks, capturable and tameable,
Finally to be perched in the niche of a Gothic room,
Picturesquely above a vase of roses.

At last one always wants to take the world inside,
Winding in the cord almost imperceptibly,

Hiding the swaying backbone from the hawk,
Shivering when one cuts into the veins of roses.

There is a kind of constant framing going on,
Fantastic, funereal, and yet fabulous,
A huge, kitelike bird brought down into the rosy world
Of calm and beauty which ceases to bleed.

The man for a moment is led to believe
He does not suffer from vertigo anymore,
This implacable subtle motion tied to his backbone,
The bird moving out from him, the roses bleeding.

It is just that instant after the hawk lights in his niche,
The roses, luxurious as lovers, settle in the vase—
An inscrutable dawn enters the Gothic room
And asks the man quite brutally for life.

The Carcass

Just an animal—much as we say of man: Just an ape—
Skinned, hung on a meathook, the head and feet cut off
As if, only up to a point, it were wise enough, just fleet
    enough, to escape.

Now that the blood is still, it is too heavy and earth-laden.
It knew that the man from the abattoir was coming with a
    knife in his hand;
That it did not feed therefore the mighty snow-white
    bull, beloved of the sensuous maiden.

The point all along was simply the point one finally
    reaches.

45

There is a statement at the end of everything, a brutal
    abstract such as:
When will the body be manageably still and dry of all the
    liquids that it leaches.

Suddenly an iridescence films the eyes that cannot quite
    equate
The puissant animal whose steps were counted in
    advance
With this most ponderous, downward pointing thing of
    any comparable weight.

And yet there is a kind of fascinating stained-glass
    window glow,
Yellow, muted green, red, purple, blue, in mashed
    kaleidoscope,
As if matter were the heaviest and the very thinnest thing
    we possibly can know.

The next time you see something powerful and supple
    utterly on the run
Give yourself up to paradox as though hanging by your
    feet, an upside-down savior
Who never could explain to heavy flesh how light and
    colorful it is filtering the sun.

Neanderthal Memories

That morning you woke and knew each organ
Had its own invincible memory—
The luxurious bed, a fur pallet:

46

That would do for the bottom of your touch.
You had drawn the shades as primal gesture;
You had smelled the leaves on the musk pillow,
Tasted a berry from your tangled hair—
Instinct moved like a stone snake in your loins.

Inveterate social climber that you are,
You ask, what, oh what, will the neighbors think?
Am I stooped beneath the sensual burden,
Do I hold the breast like a fruit too long?
Am I eating roots while they eat cornflakes?—
The body rolls in its own sign language;
Soft lip on lip goes down the steep incline
Where the first parvenus lie in a knot.

No wonder you part, separately grope the room,
Feeling for an art somewhere on the walls,
The tall, tensed, anatomical drawing—
Do tears sweat from the fingers or the cave?
One picks up the bag of flesh gingerly,
Goes with the bedroll into brilliant morning—
No one but you carries his own portrait,
Leaves it forever sweating on the wall.

Harpoon

The moment the harpoon was conceived it came into its
    own.
Little man with penknife hidden in your pocket, do not
    deceive yourself:
When the thing was thought, it was as good as thrown.

At first, it may be, you do not have the heart for that bold
  feat
Or, since you have flung the harpoon, cannot make the
  kill,
But leave it ulcerating, stuck, stalled, in that tough meat.

But you will try again because the instrument is there.
It is like abstaining from sex lying beside a nubile girl:
You care the more you say you do not really care.

What in dear God's name have we then come upon?—
A secret, nervous, two-way world of ambivalent
  connectives,
Body to body, as one impregnates targets with a
  luminously unsheathed, obscure weapon?

Nevertheless, I doubt if the fellow who hones and
  polishes the steel
Gives much thought to the thought which lusts for its
  deep mark,
Fitful to deliver, eager to assuage, above all else, to shed
  its thought, and feel.

Do not deceive yourself, voluptuous little man, kissing
  your young wife—
There is a double dark and brilliant picture always
  moving with you,
Projected so that you may stake it with a maculate
  conception naked as a knife.

Sun Helmet

The construction worker with the glistening hair
Is supple as a plant in all his thoughts,
Watering himself secretly with sweat.
His helmet, colored like a daffodil,
Takes and turns away the sun's hard kiss.
There's iron in this garden and deep, damp roots;
In the metallic light, a dipperful
Of water satisfies like jungle rain.

The structure rises but it cannot delve;
It is light rising from the worker's hand.
One block upon another mocks the glare,
The sun fights back as it has done
Since Babylon. Only a plantlike man
Can insinuate his secret power—
A passing cloud, and one remembers caves,
How the brain simmered paintings on the wall.

Under the yellow helmet, the head cools
A little, but the torso's rivers run—
What is the mix of solid, soluble?
Enormous blistering days and deep, dark nights
Contend along the narrowest catwalk,
The helmet arbitrates how high we go—
Without sun, no one ever would take heart,
A little darkness keeps the soul alive.

The Rendezvous

The woman in the white dress sits on the red sofa—
It takes only a little expertise in blurring to suggest
That she is a swan floating on a pool of blood.

The arching neck, the little white, hooded hat, the staring
  eyes
Such as might have been brought up out of the soul by a
  shoe button hook
Go with the notion of well-creamed, well-turned,
  sanguine water.

She floats on the vivid possibilities of a connection.
It is as though I had her in mind long ago when I bought
  the red sofa:
Things brim this way in the background until they flood.

Though one does not intend an indiscriminate invitation
  to the furniture-minded,
Other women came, fat as partridges, standing
  heron-legged beside the sofa,
But something placed in advance waits for the swan to
  track forward like a bird in a shooting gallery.

It takes an unassuming courage to know when the time
  has come:
All I did was prepare the pool, a blood donation given to
  the donor,
Sitting on the red sofa myself to get the feel of it.

Then one morning in the far reaches of the water
  something stirred.

I kept tensely to one side, a shadow in the shape of a
 black swan:
She was insistently a woman, and then, and then, the
 gorgeous bird.

Call in the ornithologists now to see the elegant, the odd,
The shadow and the substance that miscegenate—
I can rise, lustrous, black, streaming with the blood's
 powerful release

And go into another, quite an ordinary, room to drink a
 brandy.
The woman in white, impervious, improbable, has been
 known for years:
Spotless, detached, she sits on a sofa no one ever solicited
 for blood.

Watermarks

The rumpled pool is full of peacock's eyes,
The great bird himself a water-figment.
Long ago I saw him, heard his cries,
And thought I understood whatever his intent

Might be toward, in pride, a would-be equal and
 companion.
But those days, and some were beautiful,
Are dissolution's as much as this image in the pool—
Time has curbed the splendid notions of the gentleman.

Isak Dinesen, that great menagerist, has said,
They are proud who would love God,

And surely the dregs offered up from any soul, not
  allowed
Stringently to settle, should make Him curse or nod.

The peacock swirl—No doubt the form attracted Fate,
Harsher than God, but, in such bracing weather,
Should it be a sin, a sign our hearts disintegrate,
To grace our nakedness with some reflected feather?

5 / The Amorous Ear, The Infatuate Eye

The Neurotic Piano

She might have been a nurse in disguise, the woman in
    the long white sheath
Who came in and sat down at the neurotic piano,
Toyed with its mouth and rippled its huge white teeth.

Her round, white, romantic arms implausibly beguiled
The enormous hybrid to sustain a lifted wing
As she suckled him upon her knowledge as one might
    stuff a wailing child.

The woman even could have been the torpid monster's
    midwife—
She has come back to frolic with her massive handiwork
As if to say: When I am back in Art, I am back in Life.

Still, symbiotic as they were, and she would have them be,
The piano has an inert, oafish, recessive life of its own,
And may, like a brilliant-backward child, on some points
    not agree.

Implacable, unruffled, *tout à fait la bonne nourrice* bent
Above that mouth that she permits so copiously to speak,
Her heart could not be only full of all-unsullied
    sentiment.

There is great wit when she stands up from Laws,
Having put the wayward prodigy to bed engorged with
    song,
And drinks, as if it might be hemlock to a child, his share
    of the applause.

Homage to the Infanta

The Infanta regrets she is not alive;
That she does not still stand in her silk dress
The color of custard and nutmeg,
A gracile child at the mercy of things.
The gravid dwarf trod by the deviant courtier,
Her face like an embossed carbuncle
Which would like to suppurate the future,
And the dark, elegant, hairy artist pull
At the princess furtively like magnets;
The maids weight the pans of a pair of scales.
Behind them, a nun anxious as a widow,
Holds hands with a man like an aging Jesus.
One can hardly push through to the open door
Where a burgher stands in the slot of space
As though he commanded the lottery of life.
At one side, like a crematorium
With a thick glass door, a mirror billows
The congealed flame of a red drapery;
In the gaseous light of some harsh power

The King and Queen sit looking out like ikons.
Up front, the back of an outsize canvas
Looks like a scaffolding curiously new,
But the old, sedentary dog naps, dreams,
The mask of a fox twitching off and on—
Should we meddle here, should we invade the room
Through a keyhole like a cramped voyeur?
A stiff doll forked between a gelid eye,
The Infanta would require her funeral;
The dwarf's dress blue as a varicose vein
Would insist upon an imminent extraction—
We commit ourselves, luxuriant again,
Hazing the precise salon in blue fumes.
The Infanta regrets she cannot tell us
What she sees over our dreaming shoulders:
The tucking up of dirty underwear,
The face of a child being washed with spit,
The drunken lady who lurches and tears
Her scarlet dress as if to bleed the world,
The man fondling the phallus of his sword.
The Infanta, hardly moving her lips
In the quietest voice, whispers to the dwarf,
The artist, inaudibly, and we choke
With mimic suppositions of her words.
The Infanta encroaches where she can,
Handing us back and forth to artist, dwarf,
The maids, the man in the lottery box,
The nun with her depleted Jesus,
The dog and his toothsome dream of the fox,
The blue ikons like our mirrored faces—
The dwarf herself takes hold, reminds us
The Infanta regrets she is not alive
To see the canvas, creaking on its hinge,
Swing like a sail across a savage sea.

Nocturne for Douanier Rousseau

The world tonight is swaying on its stalk,
A dark, dark flower, a heavy bloom
Which wants to speak against the possibilities of doom
But finds itself too soporific, drugged, to talk.

Men walk around, top-heavy, sad,
Holding up their heads like melons—
They clash and dash, adulterers and felons
Who tussle for a place upon the tumbling pad.

Out of the woods, resplendent, brute,
A possibly surreal lion lopes
As if he knows just how a master copes
With such a flimsy mass of flower and fruit.

The moon itself is African tonight,
Bathes the stifled flower, soothes the vomit of a churning
    thought,
Haunts the spectral net in which a lion is caught,
And keeps its savage calm regarding possibilities of light.

Bananas and Grapes

Lying together, they might be the still-life artist's refuse.
They are cast aside. For the moment they clearly do not
    want to be eaten,
Waiting in the light of all ephemera that want to be put to
    use.

56

In the kinship of the sun, one does not wish to be
   discarded either—
Something must be done about these little, languid heaps,
Bananas and grapes, lying lazily, phallicly together.

The blue of the grapes is the sheen of a dusted flower.
You remember tulips, the clustered future seed;
Your loins perceive their spasm of involuted purple
   power.

The banana takes you clearly as its own ironic fellow,
Both speckled, amorous, both ripening rapidly—
A little melancholy when one sees the touch of melanoma
   in the yellow.

So comes the moment when you have to alienate—
The grape is on its way to being just a raisin;
Longer, darker, the necrophiliac's banana assumes its
   somber fate.

I must have brought into the world a taint,
Breathing time on yellow mound and purple cluster:
In little promise, with crucially discovered talent, I open
   up the box and paint.

The Model

She stood with her back to him like a white vase
Ready to receive whatever emotion
He might pour into her—At first, just this—
She the receiver, he the virile pitcher.
They must start as objects or not at all:

The curve of her hip felt at a distance,
The alabaster handles of her arms.
It was the liquid that would unite them,
The man carved like a troll, satyr, god.
Having placed her, as he began to paint,
Her silence would cry out, "Locate me!"
Then she would turn, mouth open like the lip
Of a vase, toward the tilted, brimming man
And a whole wash of colors would pour out
The red, yellow, blue, the lilac Venus—
So much as been said about this transfer,
The rich, brusque techniques, juxtapositions,
The man now empty and the woman full,
Her porcelain breasts alive as rosebuds,
But too little of how a man may live
Somewhat at peace without his poured emotions—
The girl walks the street now, vital forever,
Equipped with much more than she needs for love,
As though another sympathy had just
Been added to whatever contains us all.

The Tattooed Lady's Collection

When he came back from the war, I said: I can
Do anything you can, and went to the man with the
    needle
Who made me a pictured woman to live with a pictured
    man.

In bed, pressed close together, we wondered which were
    His and Hers—
The snake might sting the faun, the eagle claw the lamb:

One didn't dare to sweat too much for fear of
   inappropriate transfers.

I think he wished that mine were printed silk
And he could draw them up over my head, a filmy shift
   or nightgown,
To find the Source of Flesh still soft, white, and warm as
   milk.

Too many pictures may indeed crowd the amatory fable.
A stalwart man, blue-hung and stippled, is picturesque
   enough;
He does not want another walking gallery serving him at
   table.

So say I am set up to be Blue Lady who is always blue:
He got there first with war, a picture-laden winning
   streak,
And I, a subtle decorator, should have known to put my
   weapons on with glue.

I muffed the hardest thing to know—when not and when
   to vie.
He had fed the color on his body with his fabulous blood,
And I could only make the pictures tell his dreams an
   unconvincing lie.

The Oarsman

The long blue river was a painter's stroke
Until he cut into it and made it flow—
Nothing would do for him but active water;

59

The stalled tube was for his stuffed, silent hours.
The keen oars were like two great wooden knives
Attached to his body in lengthened sense,
The scull a case that kept slipping forward:
Two powerful incisions, and the chute,
The ecstatic getting ahead of oneself,
The scull coming back as tough, hardened skin,
The rammed knees bending up like a foetus,
The sweat on the thighs blue as the river,
The child, the man, the flowing river-god—
Of course, the deep picture closes somewhere:
The first look at the river clearly said this,
A reamed and not a stalled thing after all.
What one really wants is not knowing this,
Happy as an insect upon sensation,
This shooting forward, returning to self,
This slick corrective gaining without end.
Have you seen the oarsman carrying his scull
Like a huge dead body to the boathouse?—
The thing grew larger, heavier, in the water,
Packed with such ceaseless metamorphosis,
The blue sweat, the flaking power of the body.
The day is a flattened, rolled-up tube of paint—
He comes from the boathouse, taller, leaner:
He has been stretched as far as he can go.

Squashes

Like beheaded geese plucked to their yellow skin they lie
    in the shade
Of an obscene but stalwart little forest of thick leaves,
Lost in all that heat, in a world they never made.

60

Brought into the house they lose their murdered,
    meat-shop look—
I place them along the stone wall on the porch,
Their necks entwined like abstracts of little yellow
    mandolins accompanied by a book.

In a manner of speaking I have arranged for their
    rescue—
They are handsome as a Braque, accented by that
    important,
Lyric-looking volume with the jacket of dark blue.

Always and always the suspicion mounts
As we accumulate our world around us and see it rot
That, given the given, it is what we do with a thing that
    counts.

Which is not to say that now or ever one will quite be
    done
With whatever dreams itself to be in us at first glance,
Little glutted, yellow-bellied, murdered geese lying in the
    sun.

But if on closer look, the mandolins are warted, not quite
    so sleekly gold,
And the wind shallows through the pages of the book,
We shall have made our passions for a little while do as
    they are told.

6 / Ex Cathedra *inter alia*

The Nude Poet

All of the mattresses worn through, he lies
On a bed of stones, the ironic pea
The tense princess kept doubling in her mind.
All one had to do was live through the layers
To find that the nerves seldom entirely lie,
A wilderness of stone beneath sensation
As though in every lush feeling a pit
Fell into a quilted effect below.

Nevertheless, the body hoards its memories,
Jacking itself above the bedrock world,
Excreting its fantasies of roses,
Clinging to the splitting hammocks, loose slings—
One feels a single stone a long way off:
There is a piercing stalagmite in love;
Unknown defeat rumbles down, in under;
Death contributes the gravel from a craw.

The nude poet considers his attritions
As if the world, reviewed, stacked bodies up,
Lamina on lamina of lovers,
And the poet himself lies like the felt stone—
So this was the secret of mattresses:

The princess was no liar and no shill.
She is beside him on the bed of stones—
Thick life above them cannot hear their words.

Little Sheba

What is Little Sheba if she is not, first and foremost, eyes
   and lips?—
If the soul comes down to us through word of mouth and
   glancing sight,
Why is the intellect peaked like cream around the dasher
   of her hips?

Are we so shaken, having skipped some pages of a book,
We must retrieve the damp illumination of the flesh?—
An eye for an eye, her belly, in this guise, gives its
   deep-blind, dimpled, one-eyed look.

The barker knows the body feels the autumn night—
A cool wind flaps her stolid image on the tent:
Just as the mind goes dark, her breasts in double bulbs,
   give out their hard, electric light.

Has then the heart no certain locus anymore?—
Little Sheba bumps and grinds and makes our tenets
   wander:
Beneath the filmy veils, what deliquescent verity regrets
   the way its liquids pour?

Such expertise to make us see the bottom or the top,
Or just the middle with its soft, sight-tied, involuted eye!—
Since nothing ever came of it, what happens to the classic
   whole we crop?

Putting things together from their pieces—Was it always
    thus?
We lie on our beds amid harsh, intermittent lights, loose
    eyes, lost loci,
And bring up from this sea of parts our luminous,
    liquid-streaming Venus.

Water Polo

The muscular swimmer with the bathing girl
On his shoulders has just come up for air.
The head, close-cropped, almost viciously virile,
Blooms from the crotch like a figured stopper—
That man was born too long ago for this:
He has no second rights of orifice,
His brutal second coming stalls the heart.
The girl is almost too gay in labor.
She pounds the head as if to push it in,
Tugs at the large ears to pull it out.
Her comrades in the water do the same,
And the world seems full of ancient babies,
Radically obtrusive and recessive—
The eye says, they're only playing polo,
But the action knows another story—
The great head we wear goes back into the soul,
Or some light notion pulls it from that grip.
The grossly laden men look like tumblers—
Full of bounce, laughing, cavorting, they dive
Indiscriminately now among the girls,
Pushing up as if no one knows his mother,
Fabulous, insouciant, fully expelled,
Their heads no heavier than the water ball.

The Bodyguard

We shield it with muscles, make it so shining, hard,
Yet all the time we know how penetrably soft it is:
Each of us would, if he could, call in the bodyguard.

Not the cliché thug, the hood in black with a fat cigar:
Someone naked as we, varicolored, diagrammatic,
But invulnerable, impervious-looking as the clinker of a
  fallen star—

Someone who could withstand the furnace, having
  withstood the fall through air—
If one is going to walk around naked and vulnerable,
We want the observer to have an implacable, unwavering
  stare.

Most of us, too poor to make with anyone so exigent a
  pact,
Spend our lives exposed to colds, catastrophes, cowards,
  fools,
And never have the burnished sense of being guarded by
  an infallible, fired artifact.

He is somewhere else, indisputably walking on hot coals
As he illustrates to someone rich, varied, and powerful
That being wise means following the man with hardened
  soles.

What can we do, therefore, but be more spacious, more
  succinct,
Protect a little at a time, look far into the burning world,

As if our chronic feeling for the bodyguard were rare,
   recusant, or extinct.

Sun Lamp

Never in the sun had they found such focus—
Lamps they had been told were for solo sessions,
But how else could one make life interesting
When the sun itself had been so loose, vague?
Lovers on the beach look like meat from shells;
The sun cooks them a little to prove this point.
If they had time enough, they could gather
The light to themselves, but not in a day
Or a season. These are special lovers.
They undress as if the sheerest garment
Were asbestos, as if in some such straits
A fever blister might be a sign of grace.
Stealing the technique the sun diffuses,
They turn on the bright lamp in a dark room.
They are glad to be staked in a circle—
Never before the kiss so firmly placed,
Never before the heart stuck by the light.
They have been warned of too much exposure,
But they lie as if they have a million years
To be seen by their own close, searching eye,
His hand upon her thigh like a young fossil,
Her lips running a warm river through his veins,
As if they remembered for the flaccid sun
How tight the light was when the world was made.

The Man in the Green Chair

A retired general, a composer, a refugee from a touch
   group,
The man in the green chair is writing his
   autobiography—
One is struck with the curious immobility of recall.

One would say, in fact, that he was sitting for his portrait,
And no one can deny that he might seem more vital
If it were someone else who was treating him as object.

But there comes a time when each man does this for
   himself.
The green chair is the throne of returning dreams—
How fortunate the man looks still so bold and strong,
   receiving his subjects.

His face is bronzed, his eyes clear as an animal's, his
   figure trim;
He gives no evidence of having had to walk on coals or
   run for his life.
Why on earth has he gone so soft as this at last?

We would believe him more if he got up vigorously from
   his chair,
Left them all, the tubercular lovers, the losers, the
   also-rans,
And went briskly out to reprimand the lazy gardener.

Still, a kind of dreaming does leach from a certain wound
   in time,

Drops of the banked-up cistern, sexual effluvia, sweat
    from the metaphysical mist—
Even the face of a grasshopper may look like a death's
    head.

But it is not the end of the world, nor even the end of the
    road.
It is simply the view from the green chair—nothing more.
This is the thing biographies, auto- or otherwise, do not
    convey.

How green the meadow laps the windows like a quiet
    sea!—
Any minute now the man will stop writing, steeped in
    recall:
Twilight glimmering, the chair will not electrocute,
    indulgent of memoir.

Girl Raking Hay

In what she will look like ten years from now
I am not interested, and cannot afford to be.
She may be latent with guilt, sorrow, vice,
Lurking like an X-ray time will develop.
I want her as she is, pure and simple,
In her white dress and broad-brimmed, straw sunhat
Raking hay slowly on a summer day.
The body may have its hidden bullet
Already—that too the X-ray will disclose:
Someone she loves, hates, someone she envies—
Erotic, without consequence, I want her
As a poured-out picture that slowly moves,

Back, forth, no further than a windshield wiper,
Both proud and limited, and just for me—
She will never know how I have used her,
Heaping up my nerves in dense, tawny mounds
Her rake moves through like a thick, dulcet comb,
How I am so charged with the bright, brutal—
Mold from the dungeon, musk of sexual thrust,
A much too rapidly developing picture,
A roomful of poses, an expelled history—
One stark, tremendous contention remains,
The lucid picture that hides in the sun.
One sees it even on dark, rainy days,
Clearing, back and forth, so far, no further—
You may call it illicit, this looking,
This lying down to the rake's long fingers.
But I can only tell you that I feel
Exposed, exposed, without ruin or record,
Imprinted with something I call myself.

The Image on the Knee

Ask for that late, last sensuous friend, and you may find
    him, undeploring, undeplored,
Lifting the view of a luminous sea as if it were a golden
    cup,
Or standing, drinking wine, eating fruit at some exquisite
    sideboard.

Which is to say in knowing how to make the large look
    small,
The small loom large, he is an ardent man in any house:
Ask for that one who's been around the tracks so
    much—You find a tremulous racer in a stall.

70

He moves somewhere between the lavish sea, the lucent
    fruit—
Let him prowl, pry into your much picked-over life a
    while,
And even there he finds the nacreous or the nectared
    drop, a thimbleful of loot.

Since almost any friendship, as it wears, debases,
We wonder what the secret of this loafer, lounger, is,
And with the worst will in the world would shout in that
    pink ear: Get down to cases!

Just at that point, he shuts up shop, collapses sideboard,
    sea,
Much as a Sunday painter closes for the week his leaching
    box of paints,
Or some ventriloquist removes an image strangely like
    our simulacrum from his knee.

He has gone somewhere else—A cosier view, a better
    light—
In these days when our deliverers are late, last, and, oh,
    so few,
Someone had better go out looking for him—You go left,
    I go right.